READY, STEADY,

An Unofficial Guide to
CODING
with
Minecraft®

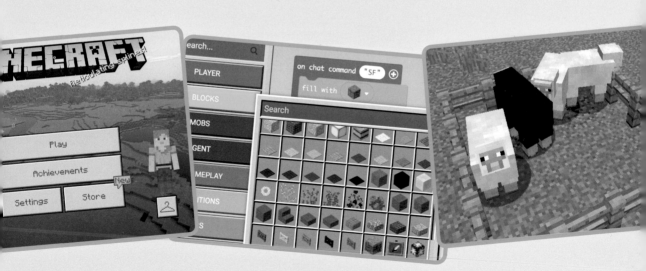

ÁLVARO SCRIVANO
ILLUSTRATED BY SUE DOWNING

First published in Great Britain in 2018 by Wayland
Copyright © Hodder and Stoughton, 2018
All rights reserved.

Editor: Hayley Fairhead
Design and illustrations: Collaborate

Wayland, an imprint of Hachette Children's Group
Part of Hodder & Stoughton
Carmelite House
50 Victoria Embankment
London EC4Y 0DZ

ISBN: 978-1-5263-0870-2

Printed and bound in China
An Hachette UK Company

The website addresses printed in this book were valid at the time of going to press. However, it is possible that contents or addresses may have changed since the publication of this book. No responsibility for any such changes can be accepted by either the author or the publishers.

CONTENTS

What is Minecraft®?

Minecraft is a game where players can work with blocks to create wonderful, imaginative worlds. The game is used to teach lots of different subjects, from chemistry and coding to literature and mathematics.

Note to parents:

What you need to work on the projects in this book:

1. A Windows 10 device with a full version of Minecraft for Windows 10 installed upon it.

2. Internet access.

Online safety

- It is important that you read Minecraft game reviews to understand more about potential risks or difficulties.

- Talk to your child about what they are up to online and keep up-to-date with your child's development online.

- Set boundaries in the online world just as you would in the real world.

- Keep all equipment that connects to the Internet in a family space. Do not let your child search the Internet without supervision.

- Do not let your child play with others they do not know.

Installation

1. Minecraft

To code in Minecraft, you will need a full version (not just the X-Box version) of Minecraft installed on your desktop computer. Minecraft for Windows 10 can be accessed through the Windows app store. This is free for existing owners of the original Minecraft PC Java version or you can buy it in the Windows app store. If you have already owned Minecraft for Windows 10, you need to ensure that you have the latest update.

2. Code Connection

Once you have the game installed, you need to install the Code Connection app which you can download from **education.minecraft. net/get-started/download**. Once you install it, run it and it should leave a shortcut on your desktop.

Now you have the full version of Minecraft and Code Connection, you can use Microsoft MakeCode to code your own Minecraft projects.

You will notice that for all the projects in this book, it is necessary to activate cheats in settings. 'Cheating' is used to customise the running of the game by connecting with Code Connection.

MakeCode®

When you open a new project in MakeCode, you will see the window below:

The toolbox is made of different menus.

Click here to see commands sent to Minecraft.

Click here to stop MakeCode running.

You can go back and forth between Blocks and JavaScript editors.

Click the snail icon to slow down your program.

Name your project and save it in your device.

Workspace
The project will be built here. Right-click to delete all blocks, format code or download a screenshot of your program.

View your blocks bigger or smaller by clicking on these signs.

Redo or undo the last step.

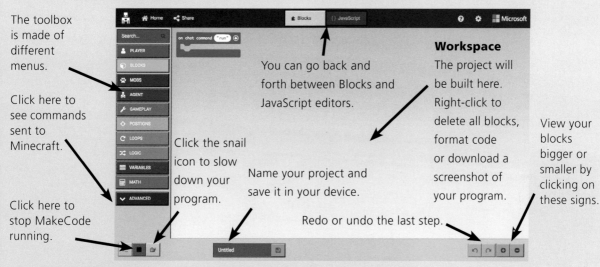

Deleting a block

There are three ways to delete a block in MakeCode:

A. Select the block and press the delete button on the keyboard
B. Right-click on the block and select delete
C. Drag and drop the block into the toolbox.

Controls in Minecraft®

The mouse controls turning and aiming.

Left mouse button

The left button is used to hit things i.e. to break blocks or attack an enemy. It will use the item you are using in your 'main hand' to hit things.

Right mouse button

The right button is used for a lot of things:

- using certain tools (hoeing farmland, shearing sheep)
- placing blocks
- firing bows (hold to build power, then release)
- throwing missiles (eggs, snowballs, splash potions)
- eating and drinking
- using the item in your 'off hand'
- operating buttons and levers
- opening doors
- accessing containers (chests, furnaces, brewing stands, etc.)

Button	Action
W	Forward (double-tap to sprint)
S	Backward
A	Left
D	Right
Space	Jump
Shift	Sneak

Tip
In Creative Mode, double-click the 'Space' key to fly. When flying, press 'Space' to move upwards and 'Shift' to move downwards.

SUNFLOWER FIELD

DESIGN YOUR OWN SUNFLOWER FIELD!

READY >>

Let's get started with Minecraft!

1 **GETTING STARTED**
Open Minecraft and click on 'Play'.

2 **CREATE A NEW WORLD**
Click on 'Create New'.

Click on 'Create New World' in the next two stages.

CHOOSE THE GAME SETTINGS

Under 'Game Settings', choose the following options from each drop-down list:

Default Game Mode: Creative

Difficulty: Easy

World Type: Flat

Cheats: 'Activate Cheats' should be on, with the toggle to the right.

Now click on the 'Create' button on the left-hand side of the screen.

STEADY

You are now in Minecraft. Don't start playing yet! You need to code first!

PAUSE
Click 'Esc' on your keyboard to pause the game.

Did you know?
Sunflowers can vary from 90 centimetres to a whopping 5.4 metres in height. They are one of the fastest growing plants, able to reach 2.5 m to 3.6 m in just 6 months.

5 OPEN CODE CONNECTION

Now go to your desktop and open Code Connection by double-clicking on the icon. You need to copy the command in the box by clicking on the double page icon on the right.

Code Connection   _ ✕

Please enter the following command
in Minecraft: Education Edition

/connect 192.168.1.76:19131

6 GO BACK TO MINECRAFT

Open Minecraft again and click on 'Resume Game'

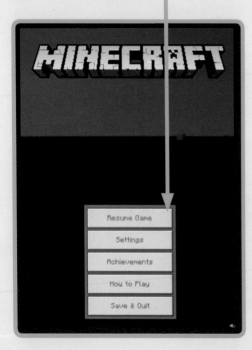

Resume Game

Settings

Achievements

How to Play

Save & Quit

Tip
If a block you drop in the workspace is greyed out, it means it is disabled. You need to ensure you drop it inside a command or function block to enable it.

Now click on the letter 'T' on your keyboard to open the chat box.

Paste (Ctrl+V) the link you copied from Code Connection in the dark grey box at the bottom and press 'Enter' on your keyboard. A message should appear saying 'Connection established to server'.

Did you know?
There are around 60 different species of sunflower that are all native to North America.

7 LOAD MAKECODE

Go back to Code Connection and click on 'MakeCode'. Microsoft MakeCode will load and then open.

8 START A NEW PROJECT

In MakeCode, go to 'My Projects' and click on the plus sign.

CODE!

Now you have everything you need to create your sunflower field animation.

9 SELECT A COMMAND BLOCK

Use the 'on chat command' already on the workspace and type in the command 'SF' followed by 'Enter' on your keyboard. This block will run the code when you type the 'SF' command in the game chat.

10 CHOOSE YOUR SUNFLOWER

From the BLOCKS menu, drag the 'fill with' block and place it inside the 'on chat command' block.

Click on the 'fill with' drop-down menu and choose the sunflower.

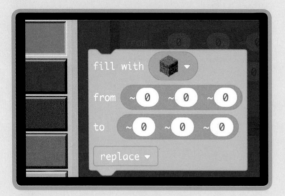

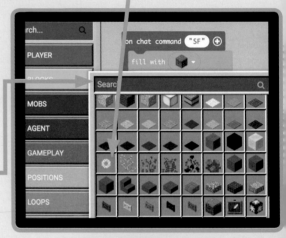

Tip
If you cannot find the sunflower, type in 'Sunflower' in the search box and it will appear.

11 SET PARAMETERS

You might have noticed that the 'fill with' block has numbers below the sunflower. These numbers are called parameters in Minecraft. They mark the first corner of the area you are going to cover (from) to the opposite corner (to). Add the following parameters:

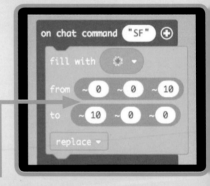

12 SET TIME AND WEATHER

You can choose the weather and the time for your animation. Choose the following two blocks from the GAMEPLAY menu and drop them below the 'fill with' block. Your code should look like this:

Click on the drop-down menu and choose 'keep' as it will plant the sunflower on top of the existing blocks.

These blocks will set the time to midday and the weather to clear.

3 WRITE IN MINECRAFT

To add some text to the animation, go to BLOCKS and drag and drop the 'print' block. Delete 'Hello' and type in 'This is my sunflower field', followed by 'Enter'.

Where it says 'of' click on the drop-down menu and choose 'Granite'.

Finally, where it says 'at' type in the parameters 0, 4, 0. Your code should look like this:

14

TEST YOUR ANIMATION

Open Minecraft and click 'T' on your keyboard to open the chat box. In the chat box, type in the command 'SF' and press 'Enter' on your keyboard. Now click on 'Exit' at the top of the screen. Move around to see the sunflower field and the text.

Did you know?
Kansas, USA is often known as the Sunflower State and the sunflower is Kansas's state flower. The sunflower is also the national flower of Ukraine.

CHALLENGE
Use your new skills and create a flower garden next to the sunflower field. Change the weather to rain.

TROUBLESHOOTING
When you run a code in Minecraft your program will stay there. If you want to run your program again, delete your old creation by mining it (destroy what is in front of the agent by left-clicking on the mouse) or walk away from it and then run your program again in a different place.

SHEEP PEN

DESIGN A HOME FOR SOME SHEEP

READY ▶

Get Minecraft open, but don't start playing!

 1 **GETTING STARTED**
Follow Steps 1 to 3 on pages 6 and 7 to open Minecraft.

STEADY ▶▶

You are in Minecraft. Now you need to get everything ready to code!

2 **OPEN CODE CONNECTION AND MAKECODE**
Follow Steps 4 to 8 on pages 7 to 9 to open Code Connection and MakeCode.

CODE!

Now you can start creating your sheep pen.

3 SELECT A COMMAND BLOCK

Use the 'on chat command' already on the workspace and type in the command 'pen', then press 'Enter'. This block will run the code when you type the command in the game chat. Type in a command that will help identify your creation, such as 'pen'.

4 ADD A FENCE

From the BLOCKS menu, drag the 'place at' block and drop it inside the 'on chat command' block.

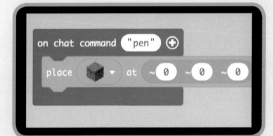

Click on the place drop-down menu and type in 'Fence' in the search box. All the available fences will appear. Choose the one you like most for your animation.

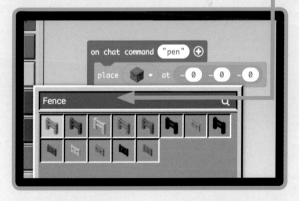

Did you know?
The bighorn sheep is a species of sheep native to North America. It was named after its large, curled horns.

5

DUPLICATE A BLOCK

Right-click on the 'place at' block and select 'Duplicate' from the drop-down menu.

Repeat this until you have four 'place at' blocks. Position all of these within the 'on chat command' block

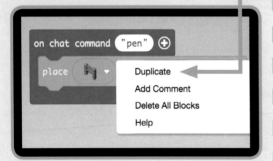

6 POSITION THE FENCE

Type in the following parameters for your fences:

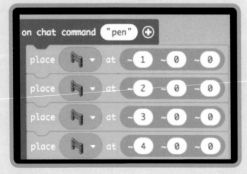

7 TURN THE AGENT

Go to the AGENT menu and drag the 'agent turn left' block onto the workspace. Drop it inside 'on chat command' under the last 'place at' block.

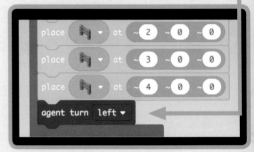

8 COMPLETE THE FENCE

Add the other sides of the pen by repeating Steps 5–7. Then add the parameters as follows:

9 TEST YOUR PROGRAM

Go to Minecraft and click 'T' on your keyboard to open the chat box. Type in 'pen' and press 'Enter'. Now click on 'Exit' at the top of the screen. Do not forget to move around to look at your square pen. Try to fly up and see how it looks.

10 ADD THE SHEEP

For this part, you need to go inside the pen in Minecraft. Once you are there, press 'Esc' to pause the game and return to MakeCode. You are going to add another command block for the sheep. Drag and drop a new 'on command chat' from the PLAYER menu, next to the pen program and type in 'sheep'.

11 USE LOOPS

For this part, you need to go to LOOPS and drag and drop the 'repeat' block inside the 'on command chat' block.

Did you know?
Sheep are social animals and they love to stay in herds. A group of sheep is called a flock or mob.

12 **ANIMAL SPAWNING**
Go to the MOBS menu and
drag the 'spawn animal at'
block inside the 'repeat' block.
Click on the drop-down menu
and choose 'Sheep'.

Drag your mouse over the
picture and the name of the
animal will appear.

Your program should look
like this when it is finished in
MakeCode:

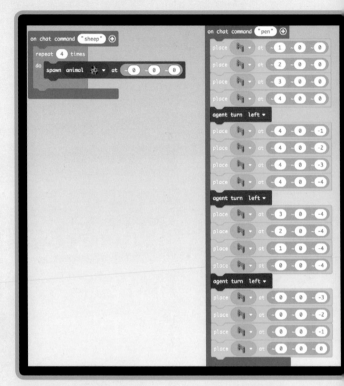

13 **TEST YOUR PROGRAM**
Go to Minecraft and make
sure you are inside the
pen. Click 'T' on your
keyboard to open the chat
box. Type in 'sheep' and
press 'Enter'. Four sheep
should be spawned inside
the pen. Do not forget to
move around to look at
the sheep inside the pen.
You program should look
like this when it is finished
in Minecraft:

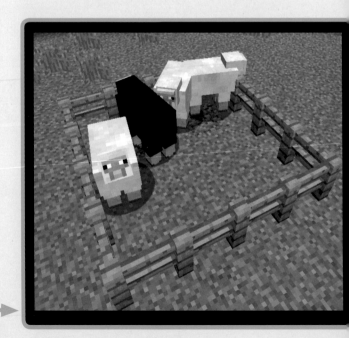

CHALLENGE

Use your new skills and spawn more animals. Add a hungry wolf outside the pen looking at the sheep! Try to change the weather.

TROUBLESHOOTING

If the sheep are not inside the pen, it is because you have not moved inside the pen first. To solve this, while you are in Minecraft and before running the command 'sheep', use your keyboard to move inside the pen (see page 5 for controls in Minecraft) and then run the sheep command.

If you think that there are too many sheep inside the pen, you need to change the number of animals spawned in the repeat block in the 'sheep' command. Try a smaller number.

Did you know?

Sheep are able to see things to the front, side and almost behind them without turning their heads because of the shape of their eyes.

RABBITS IN THE FOREST

CREATE A FOREST WITH RABBITS HOPPING AROUND!

READY

Get Minecraft open, but don't start playing!

1 GETTING STARTED
Follow Steps 1 to 3 on pages 6 and 7 to open Minecraft.

Did you know?
Rabbits can have as many as 25 babies in one year.

STEADY

Before you start coding, you need to open up MakeCode.

2 OPEN CODE CONNECTION AND MAKECODE
Follow Steps 4 to 8 on pages 7 to 9 to open Code Connection and MakeCode.

CODE! >>

Now you're ready to create your rabbit animation!

3 SELECT A COMMAND BLOCK

Use the 'on chat command' already on the workspace and type in the command 'pond', followed by 'Enter'. This block will run the code when you type the command in the game chat.

From the BLOCKS menu, drag the 'replace with' block and drop it inside the 'on chat command' block.

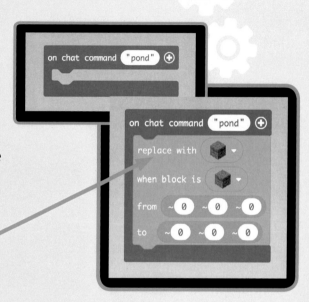

4 CHOOSE BLOCKS

Click on the drop-down menu in the 'replace with' section and choose 'Water'.

If you cannot find it, type in 'Water' in the search box. Add the following parameters:

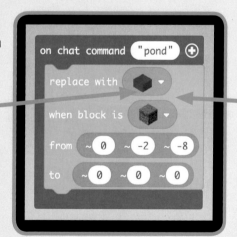

These blocks will replace the grass blocks with water blocks within the parameters shown here.

> **Did you know?**
> A female rabbit is called a doe and a male rabbit is called a buck.

19

5

TELEPORT A PLAYER

After finishing the pond, the player needs to move to another place to create other parts for this animation. You need to use a 'teleport to' block to move your player to another position. This block has parameters because you need to indicate where you want your player to be.

Go to the PLAYER menu and add the 'teleport to' block underneath the 'replace with' block and adjust the parameters.

6

CREATE THE FOREST

Drag and drop a new 'on chat command' block from the PLAYER menu and type in 'woods'. Inside the 'on chat command' block add a 'fill with' block from the BLOCKS menu and search for 'Dark Oak Sapling' trees. Finally, add a 'teleport to' block from the PLAYER menu to move the player away once the forest program is complete. Adjust the parameters as follows:

These parameters will place the woods by the pond.

Select 'keep' to plant the trees on top of the grass.

This block will move the player away after finishing the woods.

7

SET THE TIME AND WEATHER

Go to the LOOPS menu and drag and drop the 'on start' block on to the workspace. Go to the GAMEPLAY menu and drag and drop the 'time set' block inside the 'on start' block, then add the 'weather' block. Select 'rain' from the drop-down menu.

The blocks should look like this:

8 ADD ANIMALS TO YOUR ANIMATION

You will add rabbits to your animation using a different command block. Go to the PLAYER menu and drag and drop the 'on player walk' command on to the workspace. Inside this block, add the 'spawn animal' block from the MOBS menu and choose 'rabbit' from the drop-down list.

Your program should look like this when it is finished:

Did you know?
Rabbits have ears which can grow to as long as 10 cm.

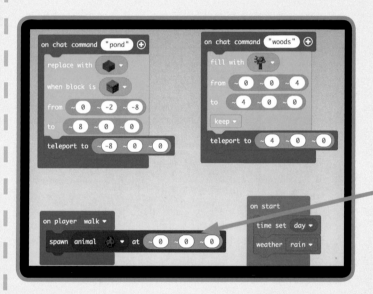

Leave the co-ordinates at 0,0,0. The rabbits will be spawned in the same place where the player is.

9 TEST YOUR PROGRAM

Go to Minecraft and click 'T' on your keyboard to open the chat box. Type in 'pond' and press 'Enter'. Then type in 'woods' and press 'Enter'. Now click on 'Exit'. Walk around and then turn. Do you see rabbits behind you? That is because your program spawns a rabbit every time you walk.

CHALLENGE

Change the time to 'midday' and the weather to 'clear'. Change the 'on player walk' to 'on player swim' block and change the animal. Go back to Minecraft, swim in the pond and see what happens!

TROUBLESHOOTING

If you think that the woods are far away from the pond, you may need to change the parameters in the 'teleport to' block in the 'pond' command. Try -2 instead of -8 for the parameters in the first box.

FARMING

SOW SOME SEEDS AND WATCH THEM GROW!

READY

Get Minecraft open, but don't start playing!

1 GETTING STARTED
Follow Steps 1 to 3 on pages 6 and 7 to open Minecraft.

STEADY

You are in Minecraft. Now you need to get everything ready to code!

2 OPEN CODE CONNECTION AND MAKECODE
Follow Steps 4 to 8 on pages 7 to 9 to open Code Connection and MakeCode.

FILL IN YOUR INVENTORY

For this project, you will need to provide some seeds for the agent to plant.

Go back to Minecraft and click 'E' on your keyboard. The inventory window will open up.

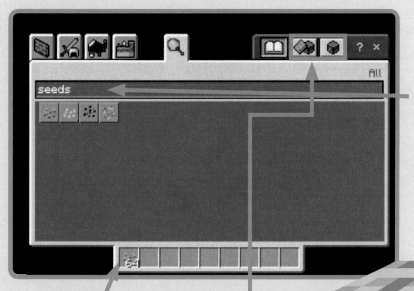

a) Type in the word 'seeds' in the dark grey box.

b) Choose any seeds you like by clicking on them and dropping them in one of the slots at the bottom of the page.

c) Then click on either of these two icons to fill in the agent's inventory, see Step 4.

Tip
If you want to see what the agent has in his inventory, right-click on the agent and you will see the inventory.

FAIRTRADE INTERNATIONAL

Did you know?
Fairtrade is when farmers are given a fair amount of money for the products they produce. It makes sure that farmers in the developing world have better working conditions.

4

DRAG AND DROP ITEMS FROM THE INVENTORY

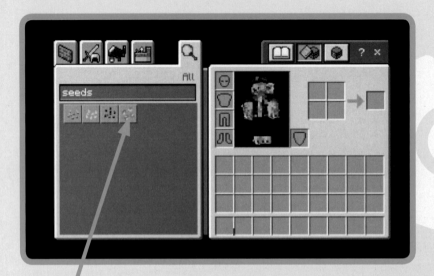

Drag the seeds from the inventory by clicking on the seeds.

Drop the seeds in the top left slot by clicking in the slot. The agent will drop what is in this slot first.

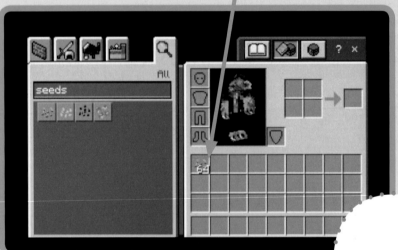

The seeds are now ready to be sown!

Tip
Hover the mouse pointer over the seeds to see their names.

CODE!

Now your agent can start farming!

5 SOW THE SEEDS

Use the 'on chat command' already on the workspace and type in the command 'sow', followed by 'Enter'. This block will run the code when you type the command in the game chat.

6 GET YOUR AGENT MOVING

Drag and drop the following blocks from the AGENT menu:

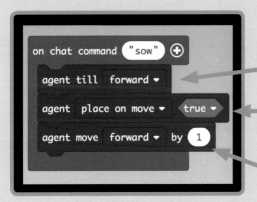

This block will make the agent till soil forward.

This block will make the agent plant the seeds from the active inventory slot every time it moves.

This block will make the agent move forward by one block.

7 TEST YOUR PROGRAM

Go to Minecraft, open the chat box by clicking 'T' on the keyboard and type in 'sow'. You should see the agent planting the seeds you added to the inventory.

8 USE LOOPS

Go back to MakeCode, drag the agent blocks (orange) outside the 'on chat command' block and delete the 'on chat command' block. Go to the LOOPS menu and choose a 'repeat 4 times' block. Drop all the agent blocks (orange) inside the repeat block. This loop will help you make the agent repeat the actions without using the same block several times. You might have noticed that the loop you have just created is greyed out. This is because is does not have a function or command yet. You will add a function in the next step.

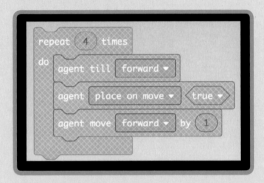

9 CREATE A FUNCTION

You are going to create a function to till the soil and plant the seeds.

Click on the ADVANCED menu.

More menus will appear below. Click on FUNCTIONS.

Click on 'Make a Function' and name it 'sow'. Now drop the 'repeat 4 times' block and agent blocks inside the function block. Your function should look like this: ⟶

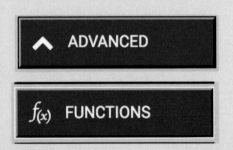

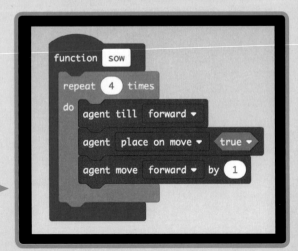

10

CREATE ANOTHER FUNCTION

Create another function to make the
agent turn.

As you did in Step 9, go to FUNCTIONS and
click on 'Make a Function'. Name it 'turn'.
Go to the AGENT menu and drag and
drop the 'agent move forward' and 'agent
turn' blocks inside the function twice. Your
function should look like this:

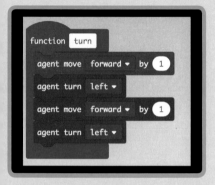

Did you know?
Fruit farming
began between
6000 and
3000 BC. Figs
were one of the
first cultivated
fruit crops.

11

CREATE A COMMAND

Go to the PLAYER menu. Drag and drop
the 'on chat command' block and name it
'farm'. Go to the AGENT menu and select
the 'agent teleport to player' block to bring
the agent to the player when 'farm' is
typed. Using the functions you created, let's
make the agent sow, turn and sow again.
Finally, teleport the player away from the
tilled soil to look at the agent's work. This
part of the program should look like this:

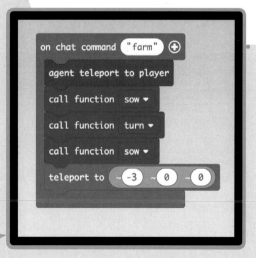

USE A TRIGGER MESSAGE

Once the player is teleported, let's change the weather to water the seeds. Go to the PLAYER menu and drag and drop the 'on player teleported' block. Then go to the GAMEPLAY menu and drag the 'weather' block and select 'rain' from the drop-down menu.

Your complete program should look like this when it is finished:

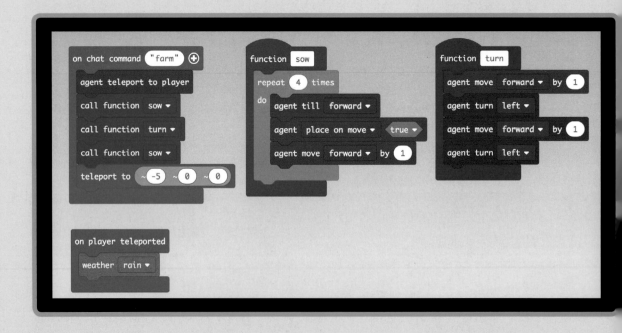

TEST YOUR PROGRAM

Go to Minecraft and press 'T' on your keyboard to open the chat box, type in 'farm' and press 'Enter'. You should see the agent planting the seeds and when he finishes, it should start raining.

TROUBLESHOOTING

If you think that the player moves far away from the agent at the end of the program, try changing the parameters in the 'teleport to' block in the 'farm' command.

```
on chat command  "farm"  ⊕
    agent teleport to player
    call function  sow ▾
    call function  turn ▾
    call function  sow ▾
    teleport to  ~ -3  ~ 0  ~ 0
```

CHALLENGE

Create another command and name it 'sun' to make the weather clear again. What blocks should you use?

Use a loop to repeat the agent's action twice in the 'turn' function.

Did you know?

Colonial farmers in North America (1610–1775) grew a wide variety of crops depending on where they lived. Popular crops included wheat, corn, barley, oats, tobacco and rice.

GLOSSARY

Agent

An agent is mobile (a mob). The agent helps players learn coding, by getting players to code the actions on the agent.

Colonial

Relating to or characteristic of a colony or colonies.

Colony

A group of people of one nationality or race living in a foreign place.

Developing world

A poor agricultural country that is trying to grow and develop socially and economically.

Farming

The activity of growing crops and raising livestock.

Function

A set of instructions that can be used to do an action.

Inventory

The pop-up menu that the player uses to manage items they carry. From this screen, a player can equip armour, tools and blocks, and craft items on a grid.

Loop

An instruction or set of instructions that keep repeating.

Mobs

Living, moving game entities. The term 'mob' is short for 'mobile'.

Parameter

A set of numbers used to locate a point on a line, map or grid. Usually called co-ordinates, they are called 'parameters' in Minecraft.

Spawn

To create players and mobs and place them in the game world.

Teleport

To transport a thing or person across space and distance instantly.

Till

To prepare the soil by digging, stirring and turning.

FURTHER INFORMATION

BOOKS

Kids Get Coding by Heather Lyons and Elizabeth Tweedale (Wayland, 2016)

WEBSITES

https://education.minecraft.net/get-started/download

INTERNET SAFETY

The Internet is a great resource, which helps you connect, communicate and be creative.

However, you need to stay safe online. Always remember:

1. If you see anything online which makes you feel uncomfortable or unhappy, tell a grown up straight away.

2. Never share your personal information, such as your full name, address or date of birth, with anybody online.

3. Remember that people online may not always be who they say they are. Never share anything with people online unless you are sure you know who they are.

NOTE TO PARENTS

It is advisable to:

- Use filtering software to block unwanted content

- Familiarise yourself with the privacy settings of your device

- Set up passwords to protect personal information.

INDEX